STARR

How I Survived Physical, Emotional, Verbal, And Mental Abuse

There Was Another Footprint In The Sand.

These thoughts are based on my perception, and memory.
I respect the fact that others may have seen the same situation in a different parallax view.

I TAKE NO CREDIT FOR THE KING JAMES VERSION (KJV) BIBLE USAGE IN MY WORK. ALL
COPYRIGHTS MATERIAL (SCRIPTURES) BELONGS TO KING JAMES VERSION.
The King James Version scriptures were paraphrased by Starr Martin for illumination, inspiration, motivation.

AuthorHouse™
1663 Liberty Drive
Bloomington, IN 47403
www.authorhouse.com
Phone: 1 (833) 262-8899

KJV – King James Version
Scripture taken from the King James Version of the Bible.

ISBN: 978-1-7283-7297-6 (sc)
ISBN: 978-1-7283-7298-3 (e)

Library of Congress Control Number: 2020917135

Print information available on the last page.

Published by AuthorHouse 09/16/2020

authorHOUSE®

Foreword

Foreword by **First Lady Karen:- Starr Martin** this is quite a work! Congratulations! You have overcome in so many ways This is what true forgiveness breeds,*deliverance and *wholeness. I think your body of work speaks for itself. You have journeyed from "broken to healed" during the course of your life time. You have also learned that abuse could be like an addiction, in that the response to it can return when you least expect it, or where you least expect it to come from. Protection is not guaranteed. You just have to learn to make better choices throughout life.

I am so proud of you! You told us the story of your abusive past about 15 years ago, wow!. I've seen you grow out of this! I'm very much impressed by your healing. I will like to also add that with God all things are possible. Your *faith has truly made you *whole. You could have given up anytime. I have seen depression, oppression, and despair turned to hope, as a result of your ministry to others. Your drive for healing prompted you to reach out to the broken, as you try to evangelize them all. Your ministry, your work for God has ministered to you. Thanks for allowing us to be part of your journey. Continue and stay blessed.

In her book, "There Was Another Footprint in the Sand: How I Survived Physical, Emotional, Verbal and Mental Abuse," Starr Martin takes you on a life's journey that helps you discover another footprint in the sand—one that belongs to Jesus. In other words, regardless of the abuse, and victimization you are experiencing, God is with you every step of the way, carrying you the extra mile. Beginning with a downward spiral of events, brought about by family instability at an early age, Starr shows how this dysfunction created a cause and effect in her home, school, and later on, in her marriage. In fact, that debilitation had opened her up to a life of abuse. In her adult years, abuse resurfaced, coming right back from the dead. Hate with its deadly venom came close to home again in a tiny village at Diamond Villa Harvest Place, on a Island called Venice.

Starr's rescue and recovery from a life of abuse, is nothing short of the miraculous loving hands of God. She invite you to discover how she was able to navigate her way through misuse, by utilizing the necessary tools she would eventually acquire, to repair her self-worth. Through the art of storytelling, Starr will uncover the principal life lessons she learned, such as forgiveness, surviving trauma, breaking the cycles of abuse, and imparting good values in the lives of children. She will show you how she applied those lessons to her own life, so that she could become a whole person, and stay free.

There Was Another Footprint In the Sand takes a microscopic view at how God used the obstacles, and turmoil in Starr's life to transform her, through a metamorphosis of miracles, bringing her from ground zero to hero. Whether you are a victim, a survivor of abuse, or care about people who are, this book is a valuable resource to bring about change, rescue and recovery.

Table of Contents

Acknowledgments

First, I want to thank God for all the talents and gifts he has deposited in me. Also, I want to give him praise for keeping me alive, well, and kicking at this time. Then, I want to bless God for my two sons, Vivian Martin Jr, and Daniel Martin. What a blessing you are, and have been. You are the best. I love you.

How could I forget my Archbishop and his beautiful wife, the faithful First Lady Karen? You are unforgettable. The interesting way you have utilized those esoteric words in your vocabulary, assures me that I have learned from the best. Thank you for all the things you have taught me over the years. I give you credit (laugh). I love you.

Marion Skeete, thank you for your divinely imparted wisdom, and instructions, in helping me to put this book together.

Much love to my dear mother, **Melda Richardson**, who has gone up to heaven. I look forward to seeing you mom, one day. I also want to thank my deceased father Hilario. If it was not for him, I would not have been able to come back to the USA.

Introduction

Starr Martin experienced trauma in her life, beginning from childhood, and straight into womanhood, because of physical, emotional, verbal, and mental abuse. But with the help of God, and others he put along the way, she was able to overcome. In this book, **Starr** will take you through her life's journey, where she encountered the full gamut of abuse. But that is not where it ends; travel with her as she take you for a ride, into her complete healing, and recovery. **Starr's** journey will teach you how to overcome the very obstacles that were, and are meant to destroy your own life.

If these abusive situations do not personally apply to you, this book can still give you the wisdom you need, to help someone placed in your path, that may have been impacted by this injustice. The life lessons at the end of each chapter, are designed to assist you, in practically applying the principles, previously explored. In fact, this publication will be a valuable tool to both you, and your family. It will trigger your mind to recognize the signs of abuse, as you interact with children, and adults, on a daily basis.

Discover how **Starr** repaired, and overcame low self-esteem, along with crippling fear. Tap into the wealthy life lessons she shared at the end of each chapter, using true storytelling, and practical applications, in addition to her own personal experiences, and victories. Take a walk with the author as she navigate her way through the vicissitudes of this life, beginning from the point of ground zero to whom she have become today, a hero. There was another footprint in the sand, as she walk on this planet called earth, and they belonged to Jesus. So, regardless of the abuse you are facing in your life at this moment, he is with you every step of the way, carrying you the extra mile.

Chapter 1

HAVING A SOLID FOUNDATION.

Starr's first encounter witnessing physical abuse between her father and mother, happened when she was a very young child. Hilario, her dad was so insecure with her mother's physical beauty, to the point that he was always accusing her of having an affair with another man. As a result, there were many bloody fights, and physical injuries, that sometimes landed them both in the hospital. By the time **Starr** was eight years old, not only was her mom and Hilario separated, they had gotten a divorce.

Starr was suddenly forced into the role of parenting her younger sister, and brother. Her mother disappeared from the picture entirely. Her father Hilario, who was a police officer at the time, was supposed to raise them.

However, **Hilario** was not always home. He was working in the down town city of Spain.

He would several times send home a bag of groceries whenever he could. Sadly, when it got to the house, some of its contents would be in ruin. Hilario loved to cook. So whenever he came home, he would "make up" for all the time he was absent by cooking for his children a good meal, that included lots of vegetables.

However, **Starr** and her sister were horridly thin, from days of not eating enough. She recalled a precious Christian woman, with eight biological children, living right across the street. **Starr** never remembered that neighbor looking mean. She was always smiling, singing hymns, and praising God. In fact, **Starr** played in her yard all the time. This missionary virtuous woman, would make a huge pot of soup, then call all the children to her table, and feed them along with her own young ones. The woman's husband was not a believer, but it appeared as though he had a very good job, and did not mind her being kind to **Starr**, and her family.

This woman had God in her heart. Even at a young age, **Starr** was able to discern that her neighbor was a believer, because her own mother Amanda exposed her to Christianity, and the bible very early on in their lives. Despite her absence, **Starr's** mother had given them, her children, a solid foundation, for which she is forever grateful. One of the most precious memories **Starr** recollects about her mom, before she left her father is this: On weekends her mom would read the comics section of the newspaper, and the bible to them, her children. It was an honorable time, one that **Starr** anticipated every week. Her mother had such a great talent for bringing those comics, and Bible characters to life.

Here are some short paragraphs (Quotes) from Starr herself regarding her present status:-

"As I sit here in this huge cathedral, gazing up at the beautiful candescent light bulbs, as they beam down on the wooden pews, I wait for the saints to begin prayer meeting, and I reflect on God's goodness. I am now a grown woman, an evangelist by God's calling. In retrospect, God was not only at the beginning of my story, but he was in the middle,

and he will always be there, even at the end of the dusty road. <u>There was always another footprint in the sand</u>. For many of you, my readers, who are experiencing a similar situation, or know someone who was, and is presently being abused. Please *know that God will rewrite that tragic story, especially the last chapter. He has the final say".*

Life Lessons: Having a Solid Foundation

Starr *remembers her mother exposing her sister, brother, and* herself, t*o Christianity at an early age.* She said, and i **Quote:-**

"As often as I think back to, mom *would send us to Sunday School. I believe it was during those times that I became aware that there is a God. I may not be able to recollect every single thing I learned there, but I do call to mind my mother personally reading to us children, bible stories every Sunday. I remember Mom relating to us the story of Daniel, who was thrown into the den of hungry lions. Nevertheless, none of those vicious creatures harmed him. God send an angel to protect Daniel from the lio*ns".

Quote:- Daniel 6:22 -King James Version (KJV) **"My God hath sent his angel, and he shut the lion's mouths, and they have not hurt me:**

Starr *continues to spea***k** - **Quote:-**

"That story applied to me. I saw how God moves in the lives of individuals. He was there in the lions' den to safeguard his prophet Daniel from being ravaged by the starving lions. Similarly, the Lord used a Christian neighbor to feed me, and preserve my life, by sharing her meals with my sister, brother, and me. She was a great role model and example, showing forth compassion, just like Jesus did when he fed five thousand men, women, and children, with five loaves, and two fishes, that were miraculously multiplied.

Quote -Mark 6:41 -King James Version (KJV) **When he had taken the five loaves and the two fishes, he looked up to heaven, and blessed, and brake the loaves, and gave them to his disciples to set before them; and the two fishes divided he among them all.**

*O*ne *of the best gifts you can give to a child is to send them to learn the word of God, or teach them yourself. The Bible gives reference of a godly mother and grandmother, who had a powerful spiritual influence in the life of a young man named Timothy, when he was a child."*

*QUOTE:- 2 TIMOTHY 1:5 - King James Version (KJV)"***When I call to remembrance the unfeigned faith that is in thee, which dwelt first in thy grandmother Lois, and thy mother Eunice; and I am persuaded that in thee also."**

<u>Starr Martin's point of view, on saving the children, and i quote:-</u>

"My point here is this, my early exposure to Christ became a bridge, that allowed me to walk through physical, emotional, verbal, and mental abuse, with a sense of hope that God was with me, even when I didn't feel his presence. The foundation to any building should be solid and strong. The same fundamental truth should also be applied, when teaching children. "It takes a village to raise a child," the old saying goes. I am speaking to you mothers, fathers, grandparents, teachers, and even neighbors. The Bible is admonishing us in:-

Quote- Proverb 22:6 - King James Version (KJV) **"Train up a child in the way he should go: and when he is old, he will not depart from it.**

That being said, there are many of you who have done just that, yet your children have strayed. Those youths will reconnect back to the truth someday. They will return to their foundation. This same God that my mom introduced me to at a young age, is the same Lord I accepted, and have a relationship with to this very day. I am now an adult, but looking back through the eyes of my early childhood, I could see the manifestation of agape love. <u>Another footprint was made in the sand</u>, as God used a Christian woman to feed, and sustain, my siblings and me. A lady who had eight biological children of her own to take care of, was still willing to care for us. The kindness of Christ was embedded in her he**rt**.

Let me say to you who are reading this book, that you are most likely going to come face to face with children, who are in a very abusive situation. You will see the evidence in their eyes, clothes, and learning behaviors. Please do everything within your power to show that child the love of Christ. You may also want to go the extra mile, by even feeding the abused children you encounter. Do your best to touch their impressionable lives with the love of God. You could save a life.

Quotes: Matthew 19: 13-15 -King James Version (KJV) There brought unto him little children, that he should put his hands on them, and pray: and the diciples rebuked them.

Verse 14 But Jesus said, suffer little children, and forbid them not, to come unto me: for of such is the kingdom of heaven.

Verse 15 And he laid his hands on them, and departed thence.

Children are very precious in God's sight. Let me paraphrase this applicable narrative. Parents were bringing their children to Jesus, so he could bless them. One by one they sat on his lap. Jesus' disciples saw this, and they began to rebuke the little ones, telling them to go away, and stop bothering Jesus. When Jesus, the Lord of lords, and King of kings, saw this, he said to his disciples, "Do not hinder the children from coming to me, for of such is the kingdom of heaven." Jesus blessed, and prayed for all of them, setting an example as to how children should be treated. Be not discouraged my friends, in doing good to the least of these in society. There is a reward waiting for you in this life, and in the one to come."

Quote: Galatians 6:9 -King James Version (KJV) And let us not be weary in well doing : for in due season we shall reap, if we faint not. (UNQUOTE)

Chapter 2

BREAKING SELF-FULFILLING PROPHECIES

Hilario, **Starr's** dad, was branded as being a careless father, and probably was not aware of how much he had neglected the care of his children, and how his mistreatment of their mother negatively impacted their lives. He befriended several women. Some of them became stepmothers to **Starr.** How long did they stay? The sad answer is, not very long. Few of them were nice. Not all these women were mentally stable.

School for **Starr** was unpleasant, and embarrassing. Her head was always leaned to one side, adjacent to either her right, or left shoulder. There were two reasons for **Starr's** strange posture. Her mom told her the story of how her babysitter left her unattended for hours in her baby chair. When her mom came to pick her up in the evening, that is what she saw. The other reason was this, during her childhood development, and environment, folks were calling her the name, "stupid." **Starr** then started acting dumb, by leaning her head to the side. The rationale for this is because, that is what she was portrayed to be. It was **Starr's** natural and instinctive posture during that period of time.

Starr Martin underscore some of the errors one can avoid, when interacting with children, and I Quote:- "One of the biggest errors one can make, whether you are a teacher, family member, or parent, is to call a child, bad, stupid, slow, idiotic, foolish, or dumb. I have seen parents even curse at their children. Harsh words is a severe form of mistreatment. Even if you do not physically harm them, it is emotional and verbal abuse.

While I was at school, my grades just got "buried into the mud." Children like us were made to stand in front of the whole school with a hat placed upon our heads, with the word written on it, "dunce," which simply means you are not smart. In addition to that, I had to hold my dirty sneakers in front of the whole school. The intent of the teachers was to humiliate. Please keep in mind that I was only approximately eight years old. At this age, a mother is expected to wash her children's clothes, and to prepare them for the school week. However, mom was not present. So my school uniform was always untidy. I remember the school principal literally giving me soap to wash my garments".

Here, Starr Martin mentions that therapy intervention will be needed, for healing and recovery, I Quote:-

"I must confess that coming to the United States of America decades later, and joining with a body of believers, elevated my self-esteem to a much higher magnitude, but the journey to complete wholeness was a tedious one.

May I interject that many individuals who were severely abused, will need some type of therapy. Unfortunately, many people end up in a mental institution, prison, on some type of drug, or sadly, death, when they do not receive the necessary intervention. Their lives become self-fulfilling prophecies, which are negative predictions, words, and expectations, that are sure to come to pass in a person's life.

The Lord has been with me on my journey, from the very beginning, or my ending would have been very tragic. There was always another footprint in the sand. I remember when I was a little girl, coming from school, I fell onto the street, and a truck loaded with coal was approaching. Thank God it was not coming towards me extremely fast, because I was able to get up in time.

The hand of God has been upon my life. He broke the self-fulfilling prophecy that was over me, predicting that I would die before my time, or amount to nothing. *It was his footprints that appeared in the sand every time.* *He had a wonderful plan for my life, and nothing could abort that plan, not even the demons of hell.*

I know someone is reading this chapter, and you think that there is no hope for you. You must have been raped, molested, and abused. You do not have to end up on alcohol, drugs, a prostitute, homeless, or dead. **You came into this world because God wanted you here**. I am sorry for what happened to you, and what occurred in my life as well. However, the Lord wants to rewrite your story, from beginning to end. He wants to give you a healthy sense of your true worth, like he did for me. I am not only talking to women, but to men as well. In a later chapter, I will discuss how I recovered my self-esteem, and how you too can recover yours". (**UNQUOTE**)

Life Lessons: Breaking Self-Fulfilling Prophecies

There is a power of resilience deposited in the DNA of every human being. It is the ability to break any self-defeat, and bounce back. It is the capacity, which allows a person to emerge, from any pool of self-fulfilling prophecy, to become what was originally determined. This was orchestrated by God himself, before he laid the foundation of the world. We are not only destined to win, but are already winners, conquerors, and indeed victorious. The reason for this is in:-

QUOTE: Romans 8:28 – King James Version (KJV) And we know that all things work together for good to them that love God, to them who are the called according to his purpose.

Therefore that painful experience that **Starr Martin** have gone through, plus the adversity that is occurring in her life in this era, *is now a part of her spiritual portfolio.* **It has caused her faith to become *unbreakable, *unshakable, and *unstoppable.**

Here are some uplifting words from Starr herself, and I QUOTE:- "Now I want to uplift all those who have suffered some kind of *abuse trauma.*

You! Yes, you are going to shine. You will become pregnant with a destiny, that will equip you to share your own story. There will be glory after this, my brother, my sister. You must fight back self-defeat, and self-fulfilling prophecies, with an awareness of who God say you are. That means, you should not allow the monster of your past hurts, to drag you down with it.

Quotes: "CREDITS" to – King James Version (KJV) Genesis chapter 37 :1-36 39:1-23 Paraphrased by Starr Martin (Joseph pays a price for his dreams, he is sold for twenty pieces of silver)

Let me share a true story from the Bible, concerning a young man named Joseph, who was hated by his brothers, as recorded. I will paraphrase this authentic history for you: Joseph was born second to the last of his offspring. His father favored him more than his older brothers, so much so that he made Joseph a beautiful coat of many colors. Joseph was always telling his business to his family, and showing off. He told them about the awesome dreams that came to him from God, one of which was a prediction that, his brothers would bow down to him one day. However, there was a price he had to pay for revealing all. The cost was hate and envy.

Let me park here for a few minutes. Joseph revealed to his family, the magnificent dreams that God had imparted unto him. I have repeated this very unwise error myself, but in a different form. On my front door is a picture image of a beautiful house that I desire to live in, plus what the kitchen will look like in the future. This little exhibit, among other things, has stirred up enough fuel to light a fire of hate, and envy **on this little Island called Venice.**

From the moment Joseph uttered his first dream, his brothers organized a scheme to plot his death. The cruelty got worse with each passing day. Permit me to interrupt this flow for a few seconds. Joseph's brothers planned a conspiracy to murder him. In my story, what I was told by my opponent was very shocking. I will not revealed what it is at this time for valid reasons.

May we proceed with this story at the point when, the brothers are deciding how to dispose of Joseph. As the saga continued, one of the older brothers decides to throw Joseph into a pit, instead of actually taking his life. Joseph cries, and pleads with them to let him come out of the pit, however, his cries land on deaf ears. Similar to this young man's story, I myself, begged my adversaries **on this little island of Venice** to stop, but my cry was futile. To them I was a robot, with no feelings.

Joseph's brothers sat nearby eating their sandwiches, laughing, relishing, in self-gratification on the revenge, they had all inflicted on their younger brother. As they sat, a group of Ishmaelite merchants with camels, came riding towards their direction. One of the brothers suggested they sell Joseph to the merchants, rather than leave him to die. He was sold indeed for twenty pieces of silver. His brothers dipped his colorful coat in animal's blood, and showed it to their father, hoping he would think that an animal had eaten Joseph. Unfortunately, that's exactly what their grief-stricken father thought. Joseph was gone. He finally ended up in Egypt. The Bible describes how Joseph was lied upon, then cast into prison in this foreign land. Nevertheless, the time for his breakthrough finally came. *It was his time to shine like gold that is tried in the fire.*

Quotes: CREDITS to - King James Version (KJV) Genesis chapter 41: 1-57 <u>Paraphrased</u> by STARR MARTIN (Joseph's interpretation of Pharoah's dream. Zero to hero.

King Pharaoh had a dream, but no one in the kingdom was able to interpret his dream. However, there were two men who had served time with Joseph in prison. Both men, a butler and baker, had dreams, and Joseph had given them the interpretation. The time came when both men were released from that dungeon. The butler told the king how Joseph had done an excellent job explaining his dream, as well as the baker's dream. King Pharaoh, after hearing that Joseph was an interpreter of dreams, immediately sent for him. Joseph had to bathe, and get dressed, to appear before the king.

To make this long story short, Joseph gave the Pharaoh, the correct accurate interpretation of the dream. His prophetic gift was finally rewarded. He was elevated to the position of governor. Pharaoh put Joseph in charge of storing all the corn, in the land during the years of divine abundance, according to the advice that Joseph had given Pharaoh. Those bountiful years, were to be immediately followed, by seven years of famine. Nonetheless, Egypt was prepared, thanks to Joseph.

Do you see where I am going with this? Joseph was being set up by God to be a deliverer, not just of Egypt, but his own family. As the story evolved, Joseph's brothers were sent by their father, to travel to Egypt to buy corn from the governor, who happened to be their brother Joseph, whom they had abused, threw in a pit, and sold into slavery. However, **Joseph had gone from** *zero to hero. Story to glory. Shame to fame.* In retrospect, just like Joseph, I started out with barrenness, but just look at my life now. I am basking in greatness, and God gets all the glory.

Quotes: CREDIT to –King James Version (KJV) Genesis chapter 42:8 And Joseph knew his brethren, but they knew not him.

Genesis chapter 43:16 – (KJV) And when Joseph saw Benjamin with them, he said to the ruler of his house, Bring these men home, and slay and make ready; for these men shall dine with me at noon.

Genesis chapter 45:1 (KJV) Then Joseph could not refrain himself before all of them that stood by him; and he cried, cause every man to go out from me. And there stood no man with him, while Joseph made himself known unto his brethren.

Genesis 45:15 (KJV) Moreover he kissed all his brethren, and wept upon them: and after that his brethren talked with him.

Joseph's older brothers did not initially recognize him. He was grown, married, had children at some point in his life, and dressed like an Egyptian. Joseph eventually revealed his identity to his siblings, who were fearful that he would take revenge against them. However, Joseph didn't execute vengeance.

Instead he had his servants prepare a big dinner for them. He wept, hugged, kissed, and forgave his brothers. He then joyfully sent for his father. As a matter of fact, he had his whole family relocated to Egypt, giving them a plot of land to live on. What was meant for evil, God turned around for good in Joseph's life.

Joseph is a perfect example of breaking self-defeat, and self-fulfilling prophecies. If he had believed what his brothers predicted about his future, and not what God said, the outcome could have been different. It is a *process* for many of us. Why I did not allowed what people, and circumstances said about me, dictate my future? Thankfully, it is because of divine intervention that I finally learned, how to break those self-fulfilling prophesies. *As a result, there will be glory in my story, and yours too.* What was meant by Satan to destroy you, **the Lord of all lords, King of all kings, Judge of all judges, Lawyer of all lawyers, Doctor of all doctors**, will turn it around for your good. *God will turn your obstacles into miracles, for his edification, and glorification.* Like Joseph, <u>**there was a second pair of footprints in the sand**</u>, walking and carrying my heavy load, and he's carrying yours too.

It is very important to break self-defeating thoughts and actions. Our adversary, Lucifer himself, wants us to live in a state of denial, so we can maintain the status quo of our present condition. He wants us to live in self-pity and doubt. He wants us to fulfill the negative predictions, our perpetrators have said about us. In this way we will accept where we are, make no changes, seek no help, thus entertaining the thought that we deserve to be abused. If you allow the Lord to lead and guide you, believe his promises, and persevere, that cycle will eventually be broken.

Chapter 3

REDEMPTION AND RECONCILIATION WITH MOM

After enduring years of abuse, **Starr's** mother separated from Hilario. She fled the scene, leaving the two girls, plus their brother with her Dad (Hilario). I know that this scenario happens in many families. However, the mother being the one to leave is quite rare. No doubt, maternal abandonment is a situation that could lead to resentment in any child.

Although **Starr** had longed for reconciliation, her sister was the one who went in search of the mother. She eventually found her years later.

Here is Starr Martin's recollection, concerning the confrontation conversation she had with her mother, and I Quote :-

"I vividly remember the first time I confronted my mom concerning her disappearance. I challenged her, asking her the reason why she did not take us, her children, along with her. Why did she abandon us at such young ages? Although I was deeply hurt, I could only imagine the anguish and guilt, that not only plagued my mother's thoughts, but held her hostage over the years. That difficult conversation when I was still young went like this:

STARR: "Mom, why did you leave me with Daddy so young?"

MOM : "I had to leave you, Gloria, and Mark because I did not have a place of my own. Your father did not come home for weeks. When he did appear, he would beat me, take all of my money, and accuse me of so many things".

STARR : "Mom, do you love me?"

MOM : "I do love you."

STARR : "Dad was mean to us, leaving us for long periods by ourselves."

MOM : "If I was there with all of you, none of those things would have happened. If I was also present in your life, you would have turned out to be somebody."

My mother felt that if she had stayed with us children, we would have turned out to be teachers or doctors. Fortunately, mom did live to see my sister pass the police exam and become an officer, unfortunately, she did not live to see my many accomplishments. However, our reconciliation began my journey of healing, though there were still many abusive situations in my future.

The desire for reconciliation is the catalyst that reunited my mom and me. The coming together of all her children would not have been possible, if she did not admit that she was sorry, coupled with our willingness to forgive her. Oh, what a sweet fellowship that followed! During her presence here on earth, she compensated for those barren years, that I experienced during my childhood. *We prayed, ate, walked, laughed, and reminisced together. These precious times will stay in my memory, for years to come.*

Mom later got married a second time to a man who already had his own home. Her husband was a quiet man, and he loved her. That house was a haven of rest for me, my younger brother, my sister, and her daughter. My goodness! That habitation was such a blessing. In fact, after I had my first child, I went to live with my mom for a whole year.

My mother sewed all our clothes, cooked all our food, and washed our clothes. She was also a great counselor, and God allowed us to spend so much time together.

She did not leave us, her children, penniless after her death, and her husband gave the house to my sister, before he passed away. Yes, God redeemed the past, as far as my mother's presence in our lives was concerned. After having such a glorious reunion, and experience with my mom, I returned to the USA. (**UNQUOTE).**

Life Lessons: Redemption and Reconciliation with Mom

Quote: Romans chapter 12:10 –King James Version (KJV) "Be kindly affectioned one to another with brotherly love; in honour preferring one another;" (This is just one of several scriptures referring to the Greek word "storge" family love.)

<u>**Starr Martin talks about deception, and the sequence of events, leading up to reconciliation. I QUOTE:-**</u>

"I am speaking to mothers and fathers, and their children. It is never too late for "*storge*" love. That is a Greek word, and it is pronounced "stor-gay," meaning family love. I can hear someone saying, "But I was not in my child's life when they needed me the most, so I am not going to look for them now." Finding your child is always worth the risk, and you may not get rejected. It's true you may not recover those wasted years, but **you can create great new memories, and spend quality time together**. Even if you are rejected, the opportunity to say, "I'm sorry," is the right thing to do in God's sight.

In retrospect, those moments with my mother, reflect how *<u>Jesus's footprints were behind me, and before me.</u> He was sweeping the pathway as I walked along.* His redeeming love was made manifested in my mom, as she passed the torch of victory, down to every one of her children.

I want to share with you the story of two brothers, Jacob and Esau. They were twins. Jacob, the younger brother, hurt and betrayed his older brother Esau very badly. My friends, before I continue relating this true narrative, let me say this. The people of this world like to say, "What goes around, comes around."

The Bible puts it this way in- ***Quote: Galatians chapter 6:7 –King James Version (KJV) "Be not deceived, God is not mocked, for whatsoever a man soweth, that shall he also reap."***

You see, we all have to believe in our hearts, that the perpetrators that violated us, or someone we know, will not get off easily, and ride away into the sunset, for a life happily ever after. Jacob tricked his brother Esau, and he finally got a taste of trickery himself. His uncle Laban later deceived him. So *please take comfort, my audience. Vengeance belongs to God, he will repay. Retaliation belongs to him alone, as noted in.*

Quote: *Romans 12:19 -King James Version (KJV) Dearly beloved, avenge not yourselves, but rather give place unto wrath: for it is written, Vengeance is mine; I will repay, saith the Lord.*

Quotes: *All CREDITS goes to King James Version (KJK) Genesis chapter 27 :1-43 Paraphrased by STARR MARTIN.*

Quotes: *Genesis chapter 33:3-4 (KJV)*

Verse 3 He passed over before them, and bowed himself to the ground seven times, until he came near to his brother.

Verse 4 And Esau ran to meet him, and embraced him, and fell on his neck, and kissed him, and they wept. (Jacob and Esau reconciliation)

As the story goes, Jacob tricked his brother twice. The custom of that time, allowed the oldest child, to get the greatest measure of his father's wealth. Jacob, the younger twin, wanted to steal it from his brother Esau. One day Esau, who was a hunter, came home extremely exhausted. He felt faint and hungry, as if he was dying. He saw his brother Jacob with some food, so he asked him to share. Jacob's response was, "No, no, you have to sell me your inheritance first, and promise me that you will." Esau was so tired from being out in the field, he did not care at this point. He said the word that Jacob wanted to hear, and that was, "Yes."

Let me intervene again here. Esau was the victim portrayed here, manipulated by his very own brother, and even by his mother, who concocted the whole deceptive scheme, as you will soon see. This is similar to my story, having been victimized by my own father and mother, then later, only to be revisited with hostility, by human beings **on a little Island called Venice.** I was innocent, and vulnerable, to circumstances beyond my control. I was only a child, who unfortunately was at the mercy of an negligent adult, who happened to be my dad. In the Jacob and Esau story, the second deception was orchestrated by these two boys' mother, Rebekah. Let me interject here, that it could cost you dearly, for having favorites among your children. Isaac the father preferred Esau, and Rebekah the mother favored Jacob. Rebekah wanted all the inheritance to go to Jacob.

On this particular day, Rebekah overhears a conversation between Esau, and his father Isaac. He tells Esau to go to the forest, fetch him some meat, and prepare it just the way he likes it. Isaac then informs Esau, that upon his return, he will pronounce a blessing upon him. As soon as Esau leaves his father's presence, Rebekah influences Jacob to pretend that he is Esau. She puts animal hair on Jacob's hands and neck, to imitate Esau's hairy physique. She prepares the special meal that her husband Isaac requested, then she sends Jacob in to his father, to receive the blessing that was intended for Esau.

I want you, my readers, to know that Isaac the father was blind. But somehow, he knew that something was not quite right. You can see that in:-

Quote: *Genesis 27:22 -(KJV), "And Jacob went near unto Isaac his father; and he felt him, and said, 'The voice is Jacob's voice, but the hands are the hands of Esau.'*

"Anyway, Isaac touched Jacob, and he blessed him. When Esau finally returned with what his father asked for, Isaac discovered that he was deceived. Esau seeing his father's reaction, knew what his brother had done. He cried out bitterly, vowing to kill Jacob. When Rebekah heard about the plot, she quickly packed Jacob's bag, and sent him running. He was heading out to his uncle Laban's residence, on the other side of the mountain.

Ladies and gentlemen, make no mistake— those tears that Esau shed that day, were heard by the Lord. Years later, after Jacob tricked Esau, and stole his birthright, God was able to heal Esau's heart. God also worked on Jacob's flaws, shaping him into a godly man. In fact, God changed Jacob's name to Israel, which also meant his character was changed.

Quote: *Genesis chapter 35:10 -KIng James Version (KJV) And God said unto him, Thy name is Jacob: thy name shall not be called any more Jacob, but Israel shall be thy name :and he called his name Israel.*

Ladies and gentlemen, the next step was for Jacob and Esau to be reunited. Esau had been looking for Jacob for years, not out of vengeance, but with a desire for reconciliation. Jacob, burdened down by guilt, also desired reconciliation. God prepared both hearts, like he did with me, and my mom. *It was the perfect time to bury the pain, and its memories. Indeed it was the season to cry, love, embrace, and forgive.* Jacob and Esau absolutely had to confront each other, after all those years. But Jacob was still pretty much afraid that Esau would retaliate against him. That fateful moment in:

QUOTE : *Genesis 33:4 King James Version (KJV) And Esau ran to meet him, and embraced him, and fell on his neck and kissed him. A*nd they wept."

God had blessed Esau so much that he refused everything Jacob offered him as a peace offering. In verse 9, Esau said, "I already have plenty my brother, keep what you have for yourself." Now that verse right there brings tears to my eyes. There was another footprint in the sand, because not only was the Lord with Jacob, he was also carrying Esau, and did not forget to bless him. With all that Jacob had stolen from Esau, God had restored much more to him. That's just what God did for me, as a result of my reunion with my mom. God is rich in mercy. He will do the same for you.(**UNQUOTE**).

Chapter 4

TAKING HEED TO WISE COUNSEL

Starr Martin fell in love with a tall, dark, and handsome man. He was very comical in his behavior, causing her to laugh constantly. That was one of the attributes that attracted her to him initially.

Rumors started circulating that Anthony and **Starr** were fighting constantly, so she sought counseling from her overseer. What her advisor told her, is my understanding that, **Starr** did not want to hear it. She went ahead and "tied the knot anyway". She thought, like so many women, that he would someday, somehow, somewhat change his ways.

What **Starr** got from the union were two handsome sons. They are a blessing to her life. **Starr** mentioned not having any regrets about that. However, **her close friends said** that Starr's marriage was off to a bad start, because Anthony did not want her to work. He was the sole breadwinner, and he wanted it that way. It was his control tool. **Her friends also added** that **Starr** always lacked the basic commodities a home should have. Items like toilet paper, toothpaste, and soap were nowhere in sight. **They said** that Anthony had them locked up in the trunk of his vehicle, where he held hostage the peanuts, raisins, and crackers. **One of** Anthony 's **friends mentioned** that, whenever Anthony would go to get anything from the food store, **Starr** could always predict what he was bringing home. It was always "his favorite foods." **Sources revealed** that the couple went into counseling, and the advice that they got, suggested that whenever Anthony goes to the supermarket, he should also get some of the foods that **Starr** like to eat as well. However nothing much did changed. Eventually he ran into unemployment. It was because of this difficult time of hardship that **Starr** decided to go back to school.

Starr gives an account of those fruitless years, I Quote:-

Nonetheless, I had to feed my children, and since Anthony wanted me to stay home, I had to go to the "Way of the Cross" to get the bread, butter, and cheese.

Starr expresses the importance of taking Heed to wise counsel- I QUOTE: -

Life Lessons: Taking Heed to Wise Counsel

With all honesty, I did not take heed to the wise counsel of others in authority, when they told me not to get involved. I still went on and did anyway. The warning signs were visible right from the start, in the form of misuse. I wrote a letter to break off the engagement, however, I was not strong enough emotionally, to follow through at that time. I am sure many of you can identify with what I have experienced, or you know someone who walked on this identical street. As I said before, the greatest rewarding outcome that came out of this union, is my two handsome, kind, and polite sons.

Quotes: **CREDITS** *goes to King James Version (KJV) Judges Chapter 13:1-25, 16:1-31 Paraphrased by STARR MARTIN. (Samson experienced defeat, but at the end he gain a tremendous victory.)*

I want to extract from the scriptures a sad tale; however, it has a triumphant ending. His name is Samson. His mother was barren, but God opened her womb so she could bring forth a special child. God had a purpose for Samson's life. His assignment was to protect the Lord's people, the Israelites, from the cruelty of their enemies.

Quote: Judges 13:5 King James Version (KJV) reads, "For lo, thou shalt conceive, and bear a son; and no razor shall come on his head; for the child shall be a Nazarite unto God from the womb; and he shall, begin to deliver Israel out of the hand of the Philistines."

Samson grew into a fine young man, and he was a champion for the Israelites. He was instructed by God to never cut his hair, because it contained the embodiment of his strength, to fight his adversaries. Only Samson and his parents, held the secret to his robustness. Without his long locks, he would become weak as other men, with an inability to ward off his challengers.

Samson became attracted to a woman named Delilah, whom he wanted to take as his wife. His parents objected to his choice, because she was a Philistine, one of Israel's enemies. They suggested that he take a bride from his own people, but Samson, like me, did not take heed to his parents' wise counsel. Just because of my disobedience, I lost a relationship that should not have taken place to begin with. The consequences that came with it could have easily taken my life, but for the grace of God.

Do you know that Samson lost something as well, for not listening to his mother and father? The Philistines overpowered him, and plucked out his two eyes. Delilah, after finding out the secret of Samson's strength, betrayed him for money. After the Philistines captured Samson, they poked out his eyes, put him in prison, and made fun of him every night. He suffered greatly. However, they did not notice that the secret to Samson's mighty strength was returning. Eventually his hair grew back. One day he asked a little boy to lead him to the pillars of the building, which was on his way to the hall, where all his enemies were waiting to mock, and torment him.

Samson prayed, then he held on to the pillars, pulling them with all his might, causing the building to come crumbling down.

Quote: Judges 16:30 -King James Version (KJV) Samson said, Let me die with the Philistines. And he bowed himself with all his might; and the house fell upon the lords, and upon all the people that were therein. So the dead which he slew at his death were more than they which he slew in his life."

Yes, Samson overtook his enemies at the end. I share the same victory, but in another form. In spite of the adversity, and abuse, that has revisited my life, great accomplishments have flowed like a river, from my life right into the neighborhood, community, and world. **There was another footprint in the sand** even now, and this divine intervention will continue, for the rest of my life.

I had a few dates after my divorce, but I knew the warning signs, and vowed to never, ever, marry for the wrong reasons again. Ladies, and even gentlemen, if there is violence in the house, it is suggested by some phycologist, that you should leave. Some marriage councilors are even saying that you, or your children, could end up dead, or hurt in the situation. A lot of marriage therapist are saying that you do not have to let your abuser know where you are hiding out, just for the safety of you, and your children. The court usually settles the parental visitations rights, so don't worry about figuring that out initially. Furthermore, I advise you to never, ever create enemies between your children, and their fathers, or mothers (vice versa). Always encourage them to love him, or her, even if they choose not to live with that parent. Why? Because your children will eventually resent you for that. Your ex-spouse is still their flesh, and blood. I often remind my sons to call their father, and wish him a "Happy Birthday," or a "Merry Christmas," or any of the holidays. I would often encourage them to go visit their dad. Alright! Alright! I know, there will always be some exception to the rule. Some parents can be very abusive. All children needs protection. For that reason, whatever it takes.

We live in a society that wants to throw everything out, without trying to work things out amicably, whatever it is. Many marriage therapist often advice couples, who are having very difficult problems in their marriage, that they should try counseling first. If that does not work, then consider separation for some time, especially if abuse is involved. If this does not resolve the issue, then finally divorce. Divorce should be the last resort. Of course, if your life is being threatened, leave as soon as you possibly can.

Chapter 5

ABUSE CLOSE TO HOME

Starr was grateful to be out of a rocky union. However, after many years of rest from turmoil, and turbulence, abuse towards her had resurfaced once more, at the **Diamond Villa Harvest Place, on the Island of Venic**e, as it was mentioned before. There are two sets of people that **Starr** have dealt with, in relationship to those who maintained her building.

The **first set** of residents included an elderly strong mother, who made sure everything went well**. Starr** said, and I **quote:-** "My goodness, it was the best of times. She conducted business in a professional manner, and was respectful to everybody. Her warm, kind, heart at that moment, created in me a desire to be around her, for a very long time."(**Unquote.)**

On numerous occasions during the winter, **Star**r would go outside and clean the snow off her neighbor's car, who in turn rewarded her, by offering a small tip. Finally, she moved thousands of miles away. Another person took over the affairs at **Diamond Villa Harvest Place.** From that day, things were not quite the same.

More than one person was involved in this whirlwind of spewing out some not so glamorous choice of words towards her, **in one of her dreams.**

Starr shares her experience: I (quote)

"For a good number of years, **I have been dreaming the same things, over and over again. In my dream** I would be laying on my bed at night, then i would wake up to use the bathroom, simultaneously the same behaviour is being duplicated, in the bedroom above mine, by someone. (Suspicion may be). After all, people were saying in **that same dream** that **Starr Martin** is a lunatic. Then i **had a second dream**, folks above me claimed that I was scaring one of their family members, every time I knocked on the ceiling. This reaction caused me to refrain myself from looking through my own front window, (So the child would not see me), since it was declared that I was causing a teenage child to be afraid. This accusation that occurred **in my dream,** hurt my heart, because it was not my intention to frighten anyone. (My rationale for a child's fear is this: If you say to your youngster these words, "That lady downstairs is a crazy person," don't you know that every time that youth sees that woman, he or she will become terrified. But these individuals didn't seem to think so). **The alarm bell finally rang, causing me to wake up from my sleep**.

Finally, **the origina**l occupants at **Diamond Villa Harvest Place, on the island of Venice** moved out, selling their apartment to the "**second set**" of substitutes, whom they knew, for a nice low price. The "second official set" came in to set things in order at **Diamond Villa.** These owners are now presently in control.

After I learned that we had new neighbors, my son and I, went out of our way, to welcome them. It was not long after, that the "dark shadows" that was hanging over the previous inhabitants, would soon trickle its way into the "new breed"

It was so weird how the same behavioral pattern was now being repeated by this "second set" of new breed. This should not have been a surprise to me. They (the second owners), were already informed about everything concerning me, before we got acquainted (**Unquote)**.

Each floor at **Diamond Villa Harvest Place** has its own cabin in the basement. **Starr Martin** was allowed to have a lock, and a key for it, by the first original owners, likewise the other occupants. This is no longer the case. **Starr** in past years, had the liberty of securing her own personal belongings, clothes, and computers, in those rooms. Unfortunately, the old way how things were done has changed.

Starr came home from work one day, and to her great surprise, the cabin doors that had locks on them, were sawed off. As she approached her cabin, she noticed some of her possessions missing, most likely stolen. No explanation was ever given as to the broken lock, and disappearance of the items. **Starr said that she had no idea who took the objects**.

After a couple of months the doors were replaced. **Starr** removed the rest of her belongings, and took them upstairs to her apartment. The "second set" of **Diamond Villa Harvest Place** inhabitants eventually put up new doors, and they put in their own locks and keys.

<u>Starr gives the reasons why she is disliked so much:- I quote -</u>

Life Lessons: Abuse Close to Home

In retrospect, I have discovered that there are reasons, and motives as to why I am being hated so much. Primarily, I am being persecuted because of my faith in Jesus, but there are other secondary factors that are at play. My discoveries highlight human nature at its worst. How can we guard ourselves against these various forms of detestation. Well, it is by understanding their motivations. It all boils down to one thing, and that is, making right choices. I will capitalize the headings of each section for emphasis.

ENVY - I am envied, and despised, because some people, including those in authority, are not ashamed to show this strong negative feeling. I know envy is such a broad subject. There are so many dimensions to this distasteful emotion. I will not attempt to explain it all. The spirit of envy has a tendency to seek out people, who are plagued with insecurities, low self-esteem, and an inferiority complex. It also comes with a covetous spirit. Personally I was never, ever, a person who delighted in competing with others. Yet i have seen many with a"copycat" spirit— imitating portions of my life, from me hand washing my car, my weight loss project, my sleep schedule, even competing with the decoration on my front door for Christmas.

Okay, I can hear somebody saying that there is nothing wrong with that. After all, they would say that, imitation is the highest form of a compliment. However, how does one explain the vandalism of that same decoration, or the damages done to the exterior body of my car? **<u>I HAVE NO CLUE. I will leave that for you my audience, and the good Lord to judg</u>**e.

This is what I will say to you my readers, no one can duplicate your talents, neither are they able to copy my own hand-painted portraits of former President Of The United States of America- Barack Obama, deceased President

JFK, and President Nelson Mandela, along with other prominent figures. In addition to that, they are not able to copy my gift of singing, and thankfully, are not able to take away the joy that comes from using that gift. Now, that there comforts me.

ENTITLEMENT - I have seen certain individuals demonstrate a fact, and that is their boldness, fearlessness, and the absence of any remorse, comes from a strong spirit of entitlement. There is no fear of any consequences. On display is a great sense of confidence. **In one of my dreams,** I remembered a sad incident that took place. I protested, and before you know it, the "popo" was knocking on my door. I must have either knocked on someone's ceiling, or hit my own floor. I am a human being, not a robot. **In the dream** there was a show of defense whenever I shouted, "Please stop!" Why all this performance of self-confidence? I will tell you why. **In this dream** i saw someone in the enforcement unit who "got my enemies backs," who share their exact feelings towards me. In fact, there could be more than one person. I have proof of at least one person. How do I know this? I was told this by a reliable anonymous source. Hence the reason why one of the main characters **in the dream** was able to arrogantly tell me that i will get arrested, and thrown in prison forever. **In this horrible nightmare dream,** my plea had no weight. My desperate voice, and sad cries, fell on deaf ears. It appears as though the objective were, and still is, a deliberate attempt to push my sanity, to the point of outbursts of anger, desperation, and frustration. The aim is to get me angry enough, so that I would shout, and do something violent, or destructive. In this way, there would be a significant amount of evidence against me, in an attempt to discredit my reputation. **It was an awful dream**. I finally woke up.

Have you ever come across people with a strong sense of entitlement. There is no guilt, no regrets, no sorrow. Just feelings of righteous indignation. It is one possessing the absolute right, and excuse, to detest another person. Even if that somebody is innocent There is no opposition among themselves, especially if they are coming at you as a unit, operating in one accord, so also is the spirit behind it. My reason for saying this is, only a few people believed my true story. I am walking in this valley of isolation alone, but not lonely, **because there was another footprint in the sand**. The Lord has my back. Entitlement is when you feel you have the rights to do something, even if that right is wrong. My Bible says in:-

Isaiah 5:20 King James Version - (KJV), "Woe unto them that call evil good, and good evil; that put darkness for light, and light for darkness; that put bitter for sweet, and sweet for bitter!"

LOW SELF-ESTEEM - Although one may appear to be confident, and seem to have it all, ill cruel actions towards another, demonstrates a dificiency called, low self-esteem. When one are among a circle of people, who have achieved great things, or observed someone doing awesome works, if he, or she, compare themselves to what others have done, then he, or she, will feel very diminished. Why is this. It is because they themselves are attaching what others have accomplished, to their own self-worth, and value. I must say this. Not every one is plague with this problem. Here is some great advice: **Create your own destiny. Discover your own gifts. Develop your own passion, of what you love to do. Just do it. Relish in your own attainment**. By doing this, one is less likely to peep into somebody else's backyard. Since they got it "going on" in theirs.

INSECURITY - Although low self-esteem, and insecurity are similar, insecurity has more to do with being afraid to be exposed, for not being as good as one appear to be, on the surface. Do you ever wonder why people put down others? How is it that they look for reasons to justify their dislike, for another human being. The truth is, the image they project themselves to be, is very small, and they are terrified that their "smallness" would be discovered, and ridiculed. By hating, and belittling another person, in their mind, it makes them superior.

EVIL - There are dark forces that are coming against Christian believers every day. Satan, Lucifer, Beelzebub, the deceiver, the saboteur, call him whatever name you want, hates the people of God. He will use anyone, who makes themselves available to him.

Ephesians 6:12 King James Version (KJV) says, *"For we wrestle not against flesh and blood, but against principalities, against powers, against the rulers of the darkness of this world, against spiritual wickedness in high places."*

However, God's promise towards his children in:-

Isaiah 53:17 - King James Version (KJV) says, *"No weapon that is formed against thee shall prosper, And every tongue that shall rise against thee in judgment, thou shall condemn."*

Evil also arises against us through human agents:-

Mathew 5:10 - King James Version (KJV) says, *"Blessed are they which are persecuted for righteousness sake: for theirs is the kingdom of heaven.*

(I am on my way to heaven, and I am so glad). I **Starr Martin**, fear no man, I can say those words with boldness, because of the Holy Spirit that lives in me.

Matthew 10:28 - King James Version (KJV) tells us, *"And fear not them which kill the body, but are not able to kill the soul: but rather fear him which is able to destroy both soul and body in hell."*

LOYALTY - The first set of tenants at **Diamond Villa Harvest Place**, sold their apartment to this second set of occupants, who is now presently in the "driver's seat". I learned that it was sold for a moderate, and decent price. So it can later be resold to bring in a very lucrative profit. Also, one person from the **original inhabitants**, works with a member of this **second set of residents.** I observed that this chain of events created an extreme bond of loyalty among themselves, one that seems to be unbreakable. The links are well connected. So you could see now why there is such a loyalty to the original owners. There is a huge financial gain. How do I know all of this? I was informed by a reliable source, during the initial move in at **Diamond Villa Harvest Place on the island of Venice.**

RACISM - Racism is a wide, and controversial subject. This is when one race feels superior to the other. As a woman of color, I have been asked the question, "Where do you work?" When I give the answer, here comes another question, "What do you do there?" Then there would be a reaction of surprise. Racism could imply that one does not deserve what they have, and achieved. Many of us are perceived as dumb, because of the color of our skin, or economic background. We are recognized as men and women, who are not smart enough to do anything of worth, such as write books, earn a Bachelor's degree, attend Harvard University, sing and write songs, and the list gets longer. Yes, I was not born on the American soil; my boys were. Nevertheless, with the help of the Lord, I worked hard, paid the government taxes, and made significant achievements. I will not apologize for that.

If we as parents, teach our children at an early age, how to have great self-esteem, and still treat others with respect, and kindness, then the world would be a much better place. You have people in every profession, that are suffering from a poor self-image. They don't see themselves as persons of worth. They don't understand that they have been uniquely made in the image of God.

Very early on, children need to be taught that they are unique, special, and no one on this planet called earth, possesses the same qualities, and personalities as theirs. Yes, others will attempt to duplicate their work, but there is no need for worry. The results will never be identical. Here are some examples. Can anyone sound the same as the deceased singer Barry White? Could anyone dance exactly like the late Michael Jackson?

Let your kids know that others may have more than them. Some people will have a better house, sneakers, clothes, and cars. However, those material things cannot, and will not, measure up to their awesome self-worth as a person. At the end of the day, when those luxuries disappear, that child, who is now an adult, because of the strong sense of self-worth, that has been instilled, will most likely not resort to violence, murder, hate, or committing suicide.

Luke 12:15- King James Version (KJV), says it plainly, *"And he said unto them, Take heed, and beware of covetousness: for a man's life consisteth not in the abundance of the things which he possesseth."*

A person's value, or worth, is not tied to material wealth. Look at the people in California, who lost most of their properties, and wealth, to the pervasive fires that destroyed their neighborhoods. That loss does not subtract from their soul, nor from their character as a great person. The material goods is temporary for this life, and can always be restored. What cannot be replaced is their soul.

Matthew 16:26 - King James Version KJV (is very sobering). *"For what is a man profited, if he shall gain the whole world, and lose his own soul? Or what shall a man give in exchange for his soul.?*

Chapter 6

FORGIVING YOUR ABUSER

My friends, it must be so very difficult to forgive the person who raped, molested, disrespected, and hated on you. Yes, you have every right to be angry. The scripture in:-

Ephesians 4:26 - King James Version (KJV) says, *"Be ye angry, and sin not: let not the sun go down upon your wrath."*

This verse is not saying not to get angry. It is saying, do not wait until the sun goes down, to forgive the one who did you injustice. Do it early. Do it as soon as possible.

For some of you, forgiving your adversaries is going to be a process, on your road to recovery. If you feel overwhelmed with such an undertaking, please go to God. He will move upon your heart in a miraculous way. He will inspire you to pardon.

I do not know if you have forgiven your transgressor yet, but it is always a good idea to confront the individual in a timely manner, before they die. Sometimes, even when they are alive, they are not willing to address the abusive situation with you. In cases when they cannot be present, many psychotherapists have advised their clients to pull up a chair, and make-believe that they are speaking to the perpetrator, sitting in that chair.

Let that person know that what they did to you was wrong, and communicate to them in specific ways the wrong that was done. Express your anger, and cry if you have to. Tell them that you forgive them, in order for you to go on with your life. Remember that it is okay to do this, because God is listening. He is standing as a witness to your act of forgiveness. He will release you to move forward into your destiny, with renewed hope, and freedom.

Matthew 6:14 - King James Version (KJV) says, *"For if you forgive men their trespasses, your heavenly Father will also forgive you.*

Every day I am coming to the realization that **God is so just; he will not ignore the injustice that has been done to you**. He will punish the culprits who victimized you. Here is what :-

Romans 12:19 - King James Version (KJV) says, (to support my claim), *"Dearly beloved, avenge not yourselves, but rather give place unto wrath: for it is written, "Vengeance is mine, I will repay, saith the Lord."*

Also, **Deuteronomy 32:35 - King James Version (KJV)** says, *"To me belonged vengeance, and recompence; their foot shall slide in due time: for the day of their calamity is at hand, and the things that shall come upon them make haste."*

God will do that for you, my friends. He will give you justice.

I know how good it must feel to your ego to take matters into your own hands, through an act of violence, against your offender. Let us be honest. Many of us have contemplated this. However, if we take matters into our own hands, we will then be subjected to incarceration. Beloved, if we allow God to penalize our violators, then that will be an awesome reward. Why? No one can put our God in prison; he is a spirit.

John 4:24 -King James Version (KJV) says, *"God is a spirit: and they that worship him must worship him in spirit and in truth"*.

With all that being said, go ahead and laugh, rejoice, just for that revelation right there.

Remember, I did confront my mother when she was alive. I wanted an explanation as to why she left us, her children behind, when she left my dad. She was so humble in expressing remorse, for what she had done. And I totally forgave her. Oh, how she made up for those lost, and empty years. She had made a mistake, but she was honest enough to admit it.

On the other hand, my Dad was arrogant when he was confronted. He felt he had done nothing wrong, and he was not ashamed to confess that. As I said, my father used to leave us alone in the house for long periods of time. This neglect took place when I was so young, and had no idea how to raise my younger siblings. This could not have happened in the USA, because the Department of Children's Services would have taken us away. My father, who is now deceased, was a police officer by trade, and should have known better. Anyway, we were still able to learn a few good things from him. My younger sister **Gloria Martin** followed in his footsteps and became a policewoman. Thankfully, God granted me the compassion, and capacity, to forgive my dad. We even communicated in letters for years, before he passed away.

There are so many good reasons, as to why we want to forgive our perpetrators. Let me give you the physical, and psychological reasons. First, we are able to sleep better at nights, without having a guilty conscience to weigh us down. Second, forgiveness gives us longevity; the body is able to live longer. Third, forgiveness is good to our immune system; it gets younger and stronger, with the capability to fight off sickness and disease. Most importantly, let me give you the spiritual reason: forgiveness pleases God. **Forgiveness is the central message of our Christian faith. God sent his Son to die for us, as an act of forgiveness.** As you can see, forgiveness from a human standpoint, is not mostly for the person we forgive, it is for us. We must let go of the pain, the bad memories, even the failed relationships. The stress and anguish, is to much of a weight, for any one to carry. We must let it go. In the long run, forgiving one another will keep one from going to the grave sooner

God has given me the grace, strength, and boldness, to face all of these "monsters", that came upon the "runway" of my life. I was able to slam the brakes on this "emotional crash" head-on, because of the forgiveness lesson I learned throughout my Christian life. Honestly, it is the holy spirit who gives one the power, and ability, to forgive over and over again. I have reached a new chapter in my life. The time has come for me to move away from this **Island Of Venice.** I am looking for my dream home. I am definitely partnering up with "more privacy". The vulnerable little girl that used to be, is now standing at a long distance, in my review mirror. My self-image, and self-worth, are at their highest peak. My conscience is clear. I have very little regrets. The Godly fear of the Lord in my heart, has kept me from living wicked. I lived the christian life well, and I am still lifting up the banner of Jesus Christ. I know God will reward me.

My desire is to live in a one family house. This is just my preference. I have no intentions of ever living in a joint apartment, next to someone in the coming future. Let me not discourage you, my readers, from doing the opposite. Living in proximity to people in the same building is not for everyone. There is not much privacy. I have to make my phone calls outside. That generally happens if neighbors are suspicious of each other. Soon there will be laws that will allow land lords to have a key to get inside our homes. This could lead to abuse of power, and control. I must issue this disclaimer. There are great honest proprietors out there in this world, who are always trying to follow the right protocol.

I am getting ready to ride off through the beautiful plains of my destiny, with forgiveness in my heart, for those who have wronged me. I can finally say that I am truly free. I am rising to soar as an eagle, knowing that the God who wakes me up every morning is with me until time changes to eternity. This world is not my true home anyway, and this prophecy will come to past one day—that the dead in Christ shall arise.

1 Thessalonians 4:16 -17 -King James Version (KJV) says, *"For the Lord himself shall descend from heaven with a shout, with the voice of the archangel, and with the trump of God: and the dead in Christ shall rise first.*

17- Then we which are alive and remain shall be caught up together with them in the clouds, to meet the Lord in the air: and so shall we ever be with the Lord.

My friends, let us continue to depend on the power of God, to create in our hearts, the desire to forgive others. Yes, the pure in heart are truly blessed, because they shall see God.

The truth is, forgiving one another is possible. Jesus Christ was the perfect example. He came to earth as a human being, to prove that forgiveness is possible. He forgave the soldiers who abused him, as he went to the old rugged cross. He forgave the mocking crowd that yelled, "Crucify him!", when all he ever did was good. Yes, others will call it stupidity. However, if we suffer here on this earth as christians, we will reign with Christ someday. There will be a reward.

Chapter 7

HAVING GREAT SELF-ESTEEM

Whenever children grow up in an abusive environment, having experienced verbal, physical, emotional, or mental mistreatment, these youngsters will need some type of therapy. These children will need to know, that what they have gone through, was not right, nor was it normal. The child must be taught what inappropriate behavior is, such as someone touching the private areas of his, or her body. Children should be told that, the abuse that was inflicted upon them, was in no way their fault.

There are adults walking around with poor self-images. They are your doctors, lawyers, law enforcement officers, teachers, etc., who secretly think they deserve to be abused. Unfortunately, it was embedded within them early on, or somewhere along life's journey, that they are not someone of worth. In fact, many people define their worth, based on what they do, or what they have, and not on who God has created them to be. And that's why they are plagued with so much insecurity, and low self-esteem.

The good news is this, having great self-esteem is a skill, that can be taught and learned. Children who are exposed to these lessons at an early age, are much better able to cope, and adapt to the injustices, that life throws at them. However, it's never too late to build self-esteem.

It is only after I came, and settled into a "Christian Assembly" gathering of believers, here on the **Island Of Venice,** did my self-worth climbed to the highest mountain.

My leader pointed out the scriptures that declared what God himself thinks of me, my distinction as a human being, based on who the Lord says that I am.

These Bible verses will be a blessing to you, if you take the time to read them, and declare them over your life.

Psalm 8:4 -King James Version (KJV) says, *"What is man, that thou art mindful of him? and the son of man, that thou visited him?*

Psalm 8:5 -King James Version (KJV) *For thou hast made him a little lower than the angels, and hast crowned him with glory and honor."*

Those verses above are revealing how highly God thinks of his creation, you and me. **We were born into this world with great significanc**e. We were crowned with glory, and honor. When I finally accepted this, I began to rediscover my true self-worth.

Furthermore, it is right here on the **Island Of Venice** where I learned the,"being, doing, having" principle. Subjectively I must first **be** what God wants me to be, as I yield myself to the guidance of the Holy Spirit. The righteousness of Christ dwelling in me, has justified my presence, worship, and prayer before God.

Isaiah 64:6 -King James Version (KJV) says that, *And all our righteousness are as filthy rags; in God's sight.*

Please note that it is the holiness of God's Son in our lives, and our hearts, that gets us into God's presence, and into heaven. It is not of human works, lest any of us should dare to boast.

Now, after you **be** what the Lord will have you to be, you must now **do** the will of Christ.

John 14:12 - King James Version (KJV) Says *Verily, verily, I say unto you, He that believeth on me, the works that i do shall he do also; and greater works than these shall he do ; because I go unto my father.*

After learning how to *do*, you can now **have** what God wants you to have. God wants us to thrive.

3 John 2:2- King James Version (KJV) says, *"Beloved, I wish above all things that thou mayest prosper and be in health, even as thy soul prospereth."*

You are probably asking the question, "What does all this have to do with self-esteem?" What I just explained to you is the godly standard for our state of being, and the source of our true self-worth. Yes, this concept is deep. When your self-worth is intact, it will drive you to be all that God has created you to be. However, your life must be prioritized correctly: being, doing, having. This concept is the opposite of the "worldly system" by which our present age is governed, that wrongly asserts that our true value is in what we do (our fleshly efforts and performances), and what we possess (worldly riches, fame, power, etc.). On the contrary, **Our true value is not only in who we are, but it is believing what God said that we are.**

Life Lessons: Having Great Self-Esteem

I want to shift gears, and get even more personal with you, my readers. I sense that many of you will read this book, and this chapter will trigger something very personal in you. I want to say to those of you who are struggling with deep insecurities, and low self-esteem: Your current, or past life situation, is not the end of the tunnel. Many of you have been tortured, raped, molested, and abused. Some of you have even thought about suicide, but you have children of your own, and you do not want to die, and leave your young ones behind to suffer. Even if you don't have children, **there is a great reason to live.** That reason is simple. It's bottled up in three words: **GOD LOVES YOU.** (excuse the capitals) Yes, I want to let you know that God loves you. He brought you to this planet called earth, to reveal his love to you. Out of the millions of sperms that got deposited, when your mom, and dad became intimate, you, yes *you*, survived! You being born was an act of God's love.

You may be in the pit of despair right now. But this is not the end of your story. **You came to earth with a divine purpose, and assignment. Do not quit.** There are people that God has strategically placed within your pathway, so they could shine their torches, in order for you to see, as you walk through this journey called life. These people are sent to help you, understand your true worth. They are often able to see in you, what you cannot see in yourself. You may not be able to recognize these people right now, within the dark maze, of so many that have abused, and victimized you. But God still has his earthly "angels" on assignment.

Many of you may feel hopeless, because you're convinced that abuse, along with the low self-esteem that accompanies it, is a generational curse in your family. I always say that the curse stops right here. In other words, if someone in your family has raped, molested, cursed, and abused you, that does not give you license, to perpetrate those actions towards another person, including your children. It does not mean that your children have to be abusers, or victims of abuse. You have the power to change your legacy.

Yes, I was neglected, and abused as a little girl, but I made a promise to myself, that I will break that curse. So, with the help of God, I did not forsake my two sons. Of course, one is aware of the fact that, our children will grow up, go to college, get married, and move out. But they should never say that we abandoned, neglected or, abused them.

Satan tried to destroy my older son, but God in his mercy stepped in, and spared his life. I feel good in my heart today. I am one of the best mothers in town. God has given me the strength to stay, love, and care for my children. He has equipped me to teach them, not only about his holy word, but how to hold to, and appreciate their true value as human beings. I am saying all this with humbleness of spirit.

You have an excellent opportunity to teach your own children, men and women, moms and dads. Educate them concerning their true self worth. If necessary, instill within them a new legacy. You must train, and alert them to be more aware, of the warning signs of abusive people, and behaviors.

Instruct your youth on how to have great self-esteem, without being arrogant. Let them know how valuable it is to make good choices, based on a healthy sense of self-worth, and a love for God. Drill into them the importance of standing up for what is right, even if their own friends reject them, and turn their backs and walk away.

I, **Starr Martin** have come to term with the reality that, not everyone will love me, nor embrace me. The following promises of God brings relief, and comfort to me, every time I read them, especially in challenging times.

Some of you have experienced the lost of friends, and families, as a result of the covid-19 pandemic. Many of you have survived the virus itself, in your own physical bodies.

Deuteronomy 31:6 - King James Version (KJV) says, *"Be strong and of good courage, fear not, nor be afraid of them: for the Lord thy God, he it is that doth go with thee; He will not fail thee; nor forsake thee?*

(Find solace in the arms of the loving shepherd Jesus.)

Hebrew 13:5 - King James Version (KJV) says, *"Let your conversation be without covetousness; and be content with such things as ye have; for he hath said, I will never leave thee, nor forsake thee."*

I am well aware of how difficult it is for a lot of people to trust in a God that they cannot see, especially after their own parents, or the people they trusted the most, have neglected, and abandoned them. However, this Christian life is a faith walk. One day you will see God, if you make the right decision to follow him now. Take consolation in what God is saying to you at this time. **He is making an eternal promise to you today, and it will never change: "I will never leave you, nor forsake you."**

Some of you reading my story, have never experienced persecution for your faith, as a christian. Well, the days are coming when you may face that. When you decide to live a righteous life, Satan will come after you, and he will use others, to carry out his plans against your life. For many of you, Satan already has attacked you. Nevertheless, I am so happy that Jesus himself prayed for us. That beautiful prayer is recorded for our edification and consolation.

Take time to read his promises in **King James Version (KJV)** John **17**: 9,10,11,15, 20, 21. **Here again, I will like to give credit to the King James Version bible (KJV) For its usage.**

Verse 9 - *I pray for them; I pray not for the world, but for them which thou hast given me; for they are thine.*

Verse 10 - *And all mine are thine, and thine are mine; and I am glorified in them.*

Verse 11 - *And now I am no more in the world, but these are in the world, and I come to thee Holy Father, keep through thine own name those whom thou hast given me, that they may be one, as we are.*

Verse 15 - *I pray not that thou shouldest take them out of the world, but that thou shouldest keep them from evil.*

Verse 20 - *Neither pray I for these alone, but for them also which shall believe on me through their word.*

Verse 21 - *That they all may be one; as thou, Father, art in me, and I in thee, that they also may be one in us; that the world may* **believe that thou hast sent me.**

My friends, whenever you feel discouraged, these precious promises in God's word, will bring life, and joy, to your soul. It will remind you of how precious you are to God. If I survived intense physical, mental, emotional, and verbal abuse, and found my true worth, you are going to come through with victory as well. **The truth is, there was another footprint in the sand.** The Lord stayed at my side, every step of the way. And at times he took me up is his arms, and carried me the extra mile.

Frankly, a lot of the tragic events that happened to me in my childhood, were deliberately left out of this book for very good reasons. But God knows it all, and he gets all the glory. With his help, I have not only survived, I have thrived.

Chapter 8

BEING A GOOD SAMARITAN

I had my share of tribulation here on the **Island Of Venice**. It did not matter what day it was, Monday to Sunday, Thanksgiving, or Christmas, persecution came.

Nonetheless, <u>there was another footprint in the sand, belonging to Jesus Christ</u>. The Lord has had mercy and compassion on me, and has carried me in his arms, on days when I just could not make another step.

I have observed a strange phenomenon. If you bring together a big group of people in one room, for some reason the liars will seek out each other. In fact, the same pattern occurs with the gossipers, and the haters. This type of "group think" behavior exist.

I had quite a few witnesses who came up on a crime scene. In other words, they heard me pleading to the top of my voice, asking my enemies to stop. However, they hardened their hearts, turned deaf ears, and kept ignoring the entire situation. They were not willing to even offer me a word of encouragement, let alone advocate for me.

The Bible describes a parable told by Jesus himself in:-

Luke chapter 10: 30-37. King James Version (KJV).

30 *And Jesus answering said, A certain man went down from Jerusalem to Jericho, and fell among thieves, which stripped him of his raiment, and wounded him, and departed, leaving him half dead.*

31 *And by chance there came down a certain priest that way: and when he saw him, he passed by on the other side.*

32 *And likewise a Levite, when he was at the place, came and looked on him, and passed by on the other side.*

33 *But a certain Samaritan, as he journeyed, came where he was: and when he saw him, he had compassion on him.*

34 *And went to him, and bound up his wounds, pouring in oil and wine, and set him on his own beast, and brought him to an inn, and took care of him.*

35 *And on the morrow when he departed, he took out two pence, and give them to the host, and said unto him, Take care of him: and whatsoever thou spends more, when I come again, I will repay thee.*

36 *Which now of these three, thinks thou, was neighbour unto him that fell among the thieves?*

37 *And he said He that shewed mercy on him. Then said Jesus unto him, Go, and do thou likewise.àa*

I **Starr Martin** will (Paraphrase) this story. There was a certain man traveling on the Jericho road, when he became a victim of a robbery. He was left half dead in a pool of blood by thieves, who had even stripped him of his clothes.

In today's world, this scenario happens all the time. Similar to that time, lending a helping hand to the victim, could also mean that your own life, and wellbeing, would be in jeopardy. Passersby, a priest and a Levite, saw the casualty, but they crossed over to the opposite side of the street, trying to avoid the situation. Another man came up on the scene. Scripture calls him the good Samaritan. **His heart was touched with compassion**. He poured wine, and oil, on the wounded, placed him on his donkey, then transported him to an inn. This kindhearted gentleman, paid the innkeeper to restore the man's health, and even promised to reimburse the innkeeper, any additional expenses when he returned.

Throughout my entire journey, from childhood to womanhood, the Lord came to my rescue, whenever I was wounded. He would take me up in his arms and carry me. He was, and is, my Good Samaritan, and this is why **there is always another footprint in the sand**. God has been preserving my life.

In retrospect, I can remember my younger siblings and I, crying while my mother and father would stab each other with a knife. Even looking at abuse is a form of mental abuse. However, the angels of Jehovah were on assignment even then, protecting us children from harm and danger, and somehow keeping us in our right minds, though we were very traumatized. The prevenient grace of the Mighty One was always surrounding me—behind, in the middle, and in front.

Even with God's presence, I am extremely grateful for the good Samaritans he placed along the way, in my life's journey. I mentioned in a previous chapter about a neighbor, a good Samaritan Christian woman, who had eight children of her own. Yet she was loving, and compassionate enough, to feed my brother, sister, and me, in our childhood years. It was the best tasting soup, and meals, any hungry child could desire.

All along the way there was another footprint in the sand. Even though we were not entirely spared abuse, we were still being granted God's love, protection, favor, and grace.

When I became a young adult, my father was living with a woman in the city, while my brother and I, were living in a first-floor apartment, in the country. My dad had asked my cousin, who was living upstairs, to throw an eye on us. However, both my brother and I, were never at home. As a young adult, I had become very independent, because I had no choice. But I still longed to be parented, and cared for.

My father later told me that, he could not sleep at nights, during this time. His thoughts were oftentimes troubled, because we his children, were parenting ourselves, while he was hundreds of miles away. It is like that advertisement that would come on American television from time to time, asking the question, "Do you know where your children are?" In retrospect, God is the one who was convicting my dad's conscience, many, many, nights.

One day it just happened that I was home. We did not have a telephone. My brother was hanging out at the gas station. I knew where to find him. My father came in a truck, driven by a friend. He told me to pack my clothes, and expressed that he came to take us back to the city, to live with him. I was the happiest daughter that night. I climbed up into that big vehicle. I had already made up in my mind that, I was not leaving without my younger brother. I directed my father to where he was. When I saw my brother, I shouted his name so loud, it must have startled him. "Mark! Come on! Daddy is here to pick us up!" My brother was also elated. He hopped right on. We were soaring, sailing to a bright future, that only God knew about then.

Not long after I settled in with my father, and his girlfriend, I went looking for a church to worship the Lord of lords, and the God of gods. Again, the Christian foundation I had received from my mom, still had an influence on me. I found a little church, half a block away. I only had two dresses, which I alternately wore every Sunday. A couple of the missionary women in that assembly, observed this, and got together. These two good Samaritans, sewed some beautiful long dresses for me.

God was "dressing" and preparing me, for a wonderful destiny.

Jeremiah 29:11- King James Version (KJV) says, *"For I know the plans I have for you, declares the Lord, 'plans to prosper you and not to harm you, plans to give you hope and a future.'"*

Life Lessons: Being a Good Samaritan

Jesus is our Good Samaritan, but he also calls us to be good Samaritans to others—his hands, and feet, in the world. I have been blessed by good Samaritans, along the way, in my journey of life. But unfortunately, my desperate cries for help, have also been ignored, by those who had the means, and capacity, to help me. As a result, I have learned five crucial life lessons, on what it means to be a good Samaritan, whom God can use, to help the abused, and victimized.

1. **To be a good Samaritan you must show love and compassion.** Whereas the priest, and the Levite, hardened their hearts, and went to the other side of the road, not wanting to be bothered with the abused man: the good Samaritan showed compassion, and stopped what he was doing, to lovingly tend to the man's wounds.

2. **To be a good Samaritan you must be observant and sensitive to those who are abused.** You must not only be loving, and compassionate, you must also be sensitive to the signs of abuse, such as the lowering of eyes, unexplained physical injuries, acting jumpy, or fearful, obvious change in behavior/loss of interest in normal activities, looking unkempt, and disheveled, being spaced out, and socially disconnected, extreme moodiness, or depression, etc.

3. **To be a good Samaritan you must help to restore dignity to the abused.** The abused man was stripped of his clothing, and left for dead. It may not always be physical, or sexual abuse. However, there is a sense in which, victims of any type of abuse, feel "naked" and humiliated. You must care for them with the utmost care, and confidentiality, being sure not to further exploit their vulnerability.

4. **To be a good Samaritan you must be willing to go the extra mile.** The good Samaritan, didn't only treat, and bandage, the abuse victim's wounds, he set him on his donkey, took him to an inn, and took care of him. Sometimes, going the extra mile means, listening to the victim, and reporting the abuse. Sometimes it means, cooking meals for the abused, and neglected. Sometimes it means, offering them prayer, and counseling. Whatever God has called us to do, we cannot turn a blind eye, or deaf ear, to the abuse happening right under our noses.

5. **To be a good Samaritan you must refer the abused to helpful resources for long-term care.** Before leaving, the good Samaritan paid the innkeeper, to take care of the man. He made a personal investment, in the abused man's recovery. Sometimes we don't have the resources, skill, or time, to bring a person back to full recovery, from their abuse. However, we must be knowledgeable of the resources in our community, and refer abused persons to places such as, abuse hot lines, safe houses, shelters, psychotherapists, hospitals, etc. that can provide long-term care.

Chapter 9

GRATEFUL FOR MY ACCOMPLISHMENTS

I began my childhood journey, in the elementary school system, with failure. The awful circumstances I was dealing with at home, caused my mind to block out any kind of learning. I was crying out for help, but my teachers failed to notice the signs. Oh, if they could come back from the grave to see me now, what I have become, and what I have achieved, they would be shocked, and surprised.

At the age of nineteen, I was hired by a wholesale, and retail store. They sold everything. It is there I learned to measure cloth. I was now grown, and living on my own. Two travelling opportunities became available to me, Jamaica, and the U.S.A. I did walked through those two "open doors" successfully. I had gotten married, and during that course of time, i was not allowed to work. It was at this difficult financial period, that I made the decision to go back to school. Initially I went in for nursing, but it was not in the plan of God for me. Neither was it in the will of the Lord, for me to become a policewoman, in spite of the fact that, my father, sister, uncles, and cousins, were all officers. Some of them are still in high ranking positions. I went on, and graduated with a degree. My younger son went higher.He followed my example, and finished college with a Bachelor's degree.

After so many years of being at home, I had no idea how to look for a job. I did not even know what to wear. I heard great things about the **Urban Initiative of Venice.** I went into the building one day, and found out that they offered free job readiness classes. I just had to register. I attended those classes faithfully. It was there that I received an artistic spirit award. The **Urban Initiative** also asked me to present a prestigious award to famous artist, Paul Goodnight, at the gala awards event, on that historical night.

I continued taking the classes. Employers came at the **Urban Initiative of Venice** to conduct interviews. It was right there that I got hired to work in the banking industry. After staying at the bank for a while, my ambition pushed me to go to a higher level. I started looking into temp agencies. I did temporary work for some time, until one of the most prestigious companies, on the **Island Of Venice,** hired me permanently. I have been there for eighteen years already.

During the famous Marathon race in **Venice**, there were tragic bombings, right there at the finish line. Many people lost their body parts, legs, and arms. The community was hurting, and everybody was being generous to the victims. I wanted to do something special for them as well. I wrote, an recorded a marathon song. The intent was to encourage, and inspire. I made one thousand copies. My job was so supportive, and proud of me. They put the CD cover on the television monitors, on every floor. Approximately three thousand associates, had the opportunity to tune into "YouTube", right there on their computers, to see my video. I was shining like diamonds that week. They also had a nice write-up of me, on their web page. It was such a huge blessing.

I had done a little bit of art as a child, but nothing major, until after my divorce. Art became my number one passion. I have developed a great affinity for drawing, and painting people's faces. **I have done portraits of the late Michael Jackson, Michael Jordon, deceased Dr. Martin Luther King, and Muhammad Ali, Former First Lady - Michelle Obama, Former President - Barack Obama, the late President - Nelson Mandela, the late J.F. Kennedy, deceased R & B singer - Luther Vandross, and the talented Elvis Presley,** and much more. Some of these paintings are in the Public Library, and the college where I studied many years ago. What an honor!

Writing is one of the things I love to do as well. I was able to write four books: (1) *Destined for Greatness*. This poetry book was dedicated to the late, great, Maya Angelou, (2) *You Can Make It, I Know You Can*, (3) *The Magnificent Stone of Many Colors.* This book is written for children. (4) *There Was Another Footprint in the Sand*. This is the most recent book that you are reading now.

Life Lessons – Grateful for My Accomplishments

I am forever grateful to God for all the gifts, and talents, he has deposited into my life. I am truly humbled. I am always showing my gratitude, by giving back to the community. Yes, there will be more books, cds, and videos. I want to say to all of you who are reading this writing, some of you like me, have done fabulous things, and others will do the same. Whatever you have attained, just know that it is your Creator, who has given you the power, and ability, to acquire wealth, wisdom, strength, talents, and other things. Dont you dare say that everything that you got, is as a result of you alone.

Please parents, invest now in your children's future. Read to your children from the time they come out of the womb. Some education professionals would even recommend reading to them when they are still in the womb. Also, attend the activities geared towards parents, and children in their schools. In fact, visit your child's school unannounced sometimes. I remember one day I entered my older son's classroom, just in time to hear the teacher telling one of her students that, he was "low life." This is a form of verbal, and mental abuse. This is why, as parents, we have to build our children's self-esteem, from an early age. More than likely, we will be counteracting the abuse, the world would be handing out to them, in abundance. Many times you have no idea, what the teacher is saying to your child. So, work with the school system, for the betterment of your child, and other children.

Oh, how I looked forward to my mother reading to my sister, brother, and me every Saturday, and Sunday. Those reading sessions were like live television to us. Remember, we parents are our children's first teachers. Yes, we have a powerful influence on our youth, but it starts when they are children. Siblings can also be taught, and encouraged to help each other. I believe I learned to spell well, through my younger sister Gloria, who had a spelling gift. As children doing our homework, I was always asking her to spell the words that I did not know, or could not figure out. She was my dictionary. Lol.

Building a solid foundation for learning and development starts very young, and is an investment in the future. For example, my mother read to us so much. Every time Christmas came around and she asked me what I wanted, I would say, "Mom, buy me a story book." So it is not surprising that I developed a love for reading, learning, and the gift of writing.

Chapter 10

STRENGTH FOR THE JOURNEY

This chapter is dedicated to a body of believers, the *ecclesia,* known as the called-out ones. I am specifically referring to my local assembly.We are part of the universal church of Jesus Christ. It is in this congregation that I have been worshipping God for all these years.They have been an important part of my journey, and development. I have shared with you in an earlier chapter about the terrible dreams i have been repeatedly experiencing. This is one of them. A nightmare that makes me want to wake up from my sleep. **This is the dream:-** Every morning, as I take my shower, someone above my bedroom goes into their bathtub exactly above my own. They would simultaneously hops into their shower, as I hop into my shower. Then this person marches in a defiant, delightful manner, as they directs their hatred towards me. This has been going on non-stop for a number of years. God woke me up many mornings, so I could catch the early train, and be on time for work. I am praying that when I leave the **"Island of Venice"**, that I will stop having these bad dreams. For what the enemy has meant for evil, God has turned it around for my good. My faith has been greatly increased, so is my prayer life, because of these circumstances. I mentioned my congregation, because it is right here, mingling with the saints, that I have been able to survive this **demonic attack**. I have felt so much encouragement in our gatherings, as we worship, fellowship, share, and receive the word. But I have also learned that my strength is not in just *going* to a building, but it is in *being* the church. Many times I felt the very presence of evil, emanating from my nearby surroundings. Therefore, I have learned to "plead the blood of Jesus" every morning. For some of you who have not been exposed to Christianity, you will understand this phrase someday. In short, it is a way to pray protection over yourself, and your family.

Also, I am particularly grateful for my Bishop and his wife. What an intelligent and brilliant man, and his lovely educated First Lady, Karen. The "godly wisdom" that resides in him, is what got us into this beautiful edifice.

I have never, really, shared in details, what I am going through, in relationship to the awful situation, occurring in my life at this time, to the Bishop. Although I know he would be understanding, I always felt that he has his own problems, to keep him occupied. However, I asked God this question many times. "God, did you ever revealed to my Archbishop, concerning this dangerous situation that I am trapped in?" The reality is this, on the **"Island Of Venice"**, I was always getting threats. **Satan would say** "I will have you locked up in a mental home". The "popo" will come, and believe every word. The Popo will ask me if I want to ride in the ambulance, to go get checked out. They would ask me, "What year is it"? "What day is this"? "What month is this"?

Thankfully, there have been other believers, that I have been able to share with, who are praying for me. Sometimes, people going through abuse, are not always willing to share, so as not to burden others. I am not recommending that, as the Bible says, we should bear one another's burdens.

(Galatians 6:2)- King James Version (KJV)"*Bear ye one another's burdens, and so fulfill the law of Christ.*"

The damages that took place in my apartment, at **Diamond Villa Harvest Place,** was due to two floods, that occurred on one of the floors. This situations posed a challenge for me, trying to leave this building. I needed to repair those damages first. What followed, created a domino effect. Water came all the way down to each adjacent floor. For some of you who are wondering if I had insurance—I had none. **God had "one last move to make on my chess board."** He miraculously sent the funding for me to have the damages fixed, through a law firm. I must say that additional funds became available, down through the years. It will not be too long before I move out of this place, and it will definitely be in God's perfect timing.

I have learned so much from the word of God, as the archbishop makes the scriptures quite simple, for us to grasp. Jesus spoke in parables, but the explanations were always simple. We also have other capable teachers as well. They teach our "Victorious Living" classes. Archbishop has many other gifts, one of them is the ability to attract the attention of his listeners, through the anointing, and his own sense of humor. The atmosphere is never boring, especially when he is preaching, the choir is singing, and the dancers are dancing. I am delighted to mention our Thanksgiving, Christmas, and Candlelight Service every year. What remarkable events.

There were many unpleasant circumstances that took place in our Archbishop's life. Those trials, and afflictions, could have caused him to become bitter, commit suicide, or turn his back on God. Yet, he fell in love with God even more, just like Job of the bible. Since Archbishop showed us this example, I want to copy that same attitude.

First Lady Karen likes adventure. We always have magnificent times, whenever all the ladies get together. Some of the topics she addressed, include self-esteem, nutrition, mental health, health care, outreach, (evangelism) and much more. First Lady has organized several trips, both near and far. Not only did these travel events brought us women closer together in a bond, it helps me cope with the pain, of what I am going through.

I am repeating myself again. I get the same bad dreams, night after night, and I would find myself praying to wake up. I know that this will surely come to an end. The knowledge of Satan's schemes in my life is real. But the power of God inside of me, is even more real, because greater is he that is in me, than he that is in the world

(1 John 4:4).- King James Version (KJV) "*Ye are of God, little children, and have overcome them: because greater is he that is in you, than he that is in the world.*"

The battle continues to rage, but I am standing stronger now than I've ever been. I am a seasoned soldier. now— having done all I can, I still stand.

Life Lessons: Strength for the Journey

In closing I can say that, if there is one life lesson that I have learned, that summarizes all the other life lessons, is that the strength to overcome abuse, is realized in discovering the strength of God. Finding strength in God means, developing an intimate relationship with him, through prayer. Also, let me emphasize that by "overcoming," I don't just mean that you escape the abuse. I'm speaking about moving into complete healing and recovery. I am talking about, releasing the emotional baggage, that weigh you down. We must lay aside every weight, and the sin that so easily entangles us

(Hebrews 12:1)- King James Version (KJV) *Wherefore seeing we also are compassed about with so great a cloud of witnesses, let us lay aside every weight, and the sin which doth so easily beset us, and let us run with patience the race that is set before us."*

In so doing, we are able to run this race of life with perseverance, knowing that even when we stumble, and fall, Jesus is there to pick us up, bandage our wounds, and carry us in his arms.

Finding strength for the journey also means, finding a community of faith. If you are in the midst of an abusive ordeal, isolating yourself from your loved ones, family, friends and your assembly, can lead you on a dangerous path. You will need a circle of people who got your back. These are individuals who care, and who you can confidently confide in, and who are willing to keep you in prayer at all times.

Although we must teach our children the warning signs of abuse, and know them ourselves, the truth is, there are some things we will face in life that are unavoidable.

Romans 8:28- King James Version (KJV*) And we know that all things work together for good to them that love God, to them who are the called according to his purpose.*

However, the scripture above reminds us that, God causes all things to work together for good, for those who love him, to them who are the called according to his purpose. Also, we are reassured that, although many are the afflictions of the righteous, God will deliver us out of them all.

(Psalm 34:19).- King James Version (KJV) *Many are the afflictions of the righteous: but the Lord deliverer him out of them all.*

Be encouraged my friends. You can go from strength to strength, with the help of the Lord.

You can survive, and eventually thrive past your trauma, breaking the cycles of abuse, and self-fulfilling prophecies. This will enable you to impart good values in the lives of children, and others you meet in your life's journey.

There will always be another footprint in the sand, when you are to weary, or wounded to continue on. And it will belong to Jesus. Yes, Jesus is not just with you every step of the way. He is willing, and able to carry you the extra mile. *You ain't heavy, you are his child.*

Poetry dedicated to "GEORGE FLOYD," and all those who fell victim to, abuse violence.

CHANGE IS GOING TO COME

Lord, you knew what you were doing when you created me this way.
It was your choice to make right from the start
I made my grand entry into this world on that special day.
You already knew way back in time.
That one day I would come across the face of hate.
Just for the colour of my skin.
Could you imagine, the shape of my chin.
We lift up our voices as one, a signal of unity.
Standing up for justice, in the middle of this pandemic.
Lifting up the banner of honor, to this vast display of black and white integrity.

Lord, you did not care what the majority say.
In your mind black is solid gold, diamonds, rubies, potters clay.
Black was never uttered from your mouth, yet it appeared on the pages of a dictionary.
This is a race that broke barriers, traveling on the plains of the ordinary.
Yet a particular class of unique people, that superceded the extraordinary.

This colour represents the rich soil that covers a good portion of the earth.
Lord you caused significance in our lives, mothers of the world are giving birth.
We are built with an inner layer of resilience.
Coming back out strong, with a spirit of perseverance.
This is the set time to go forth.
Marching through the streets of Zion.
Crying aloud for great change in our
communities, and the world.
How courageous, strong and bold you are like a roaring lion.

God, did you know that we thy people were going to be abused.
Did you know that we would one day be scorned, shunned, and misused.
Lord did you know that many lives would be shaken, and taken.
If black lives matter.
Black lives do matter.
Why can I not breathe?
Why can I not see?
Why can I not feel?
Why can I not walk?
Why can I not run?

I must do whatever it takes to keep this hope alive.
Change is on its way. Change is going to arrive.

I cried out "stop", but my voice had no weight.
I told you that I could not breathe, but you did not listen.
My voice uttered these words "I cannot see".
You still did not hear my plea.
Black is strong and willing to fight
For the moral principles that is so right.
We shine our torches as a guiding light.
For all reflection of light came from God himself.
Seeing, and creating changes
To behold is such a beautiful sight.

As a mother, my heart bleeds for my seed.
Those hateful images on social media I see.
They have a tendency to disturb my sleep.
My tears flow from the pain that is inside.
Lord you are the perfect place for anyone to hide.

This world is filled with so much pain.
I will never be the same again.
I pray for you everyday my sons and daughters.
Prayers that have become incense.
Ascending up to the most high with true essence.
My sacrifices will reap the profit of gain.
Investing time wisely will never go in vain.
Heaven is waiting with her arms open wide.
To welcome her children with joy, love, and pride.
Written by **Starr Martin**.